Awaken the Goddess Within

A Journey of Healing and Alignment

Discover Your Purpose, Embrace Your Power, and Heal Your Soul

A SELF-HELP AFFIRMATION BOOK FOR PERSONAL GROWTH

ARI J.

Awaken the Goddess Within: A Journey of Healing and Alignment

Discover Your Purpose, Embrace Your Power, and Heal Your Soul

A Self-Help Affirmation Book for Personal Growth

ARI J.

Copyright © 2024 by Ari J.
All rights reserved. No part of this book may be reproduced, distributed, or transmitted in any form or by any means without prior written permission from the author, except for brief quotations used in reviews or critical analysis.

CONTENTS

INTRODUCTION	1
HOW TO USE THIS BOOK	3
PART 1: Affirmations on Life's Ups and Downs	5
PART 2: Affirmations on the Inner Child	17
PART 3: Affirmations on Growth	28
PART 4: Affirmations on Trauma and Resilience	39
PART 5: Affirmations on Healing	50
PART 6: Affirmations on Confidence	61
PART 7: Affirmations on Evolving	72
PART 8: Affirmations on Manifesting Your Dream Life	83
PART 9: Affirmations on Holistic Living and Self-Care	94
MINDFUL PRACTICES	105
FORGIVENESS LETTERS	108
LETTER TO YOUR HIGHER SELF	109
ESSENTIAL PRAYERS	110
ABOUT THE AUTHOR	115
THANK YOU NOTE	116
NOTES	

INTRODUCTION

First, I want to welcome you to the beginning of a transformative journey of growth. We live in a world where suppressing emotions and avoiding self-discovery are often the norm. But here you are, choosing a different path—the path to uncovering your true self. I want you to know how sincerely proud I am of you for taking this brave step towards self-discovery. Life may be a maze, but it is undoubtedly amazing.

With this transformative self-help book, you are taking matters into your own hands, learning to walk in your power. Growth and evolution are daily practices, but every single step forward will lead to extraordinary rewards and a life filled with purpose and fulfillment. Let me be the first to tell you: no matter what challenges you face, you can and will overcome them. By picking up this book, you have already taken a conscious step to change your life and enhance your overall well-being.

I'll share something personal: my life has had its fair share of curveballs. Before I embraced self-discovery and personal development, I allowed everything to trigger me, unintentionally giving away my power. But one day, I decided: no more. So, never think you are alone on this journey. I'm here, cheering you on through life's ups and downs.

I've been on my spiritual journey for as long as I can remember, even before I fully understood what it was. There were times when I was aligned, and others when I stumbled. But guess what? That's life. Don't beat yourself up if you fall back into old habits. Instead, acknowledge those moments and work through them gracefully, fully embodying your goddess energy. Personal development isn't always pretty—it's beautifully messy.

It takes immense courage to face the darkest parts of yourself and actively work towards healing, but I'm here to remind you that anything is possible when you believe in yourself. If you ever need a boost, return to this book for guidance and relief. Always remember: your thoughts, emotions, and actions shape your reality. So, it's essential to remove limiting beliefs, actively seek change, and embrace evolution in your daily life.

Love yourself deeply and completely, without seeking validation from anyone. Balance your goddess energy and walk in your power like the divine being you are. Your past doesn't define you. All you truly have is now, and that's the most beautiful thing. Right now, you have the power to heal, to thrive, and to step into your purpose.

It's your time to shine. Step into your greatness with grace. Be grateful for what you have now and for what's to come.

With so much love and gratitude,
—Ariyanna

How To Use This Book

Welcome to your journey of transformation and self-discovery! This book is thoughtfully structured into sections designed to guide you through the stages of healing, growth, and thriving. Each affirmation is accompanied by meaningful context to deepen your understanding, along with a reflection prompt to help you apply the lessons to your life.

Here's how to get the most out of this book:

Start Where You Feel Called

While this book is designed to flow from healing to evolution and thriving, you are welcome to begin with the section that resonates most with your current needs. Trust your intuition—it will guide you to what you need to hear most.

Explore the Sections in Depth

Each section builds on the previous one, encouraging you to heal deeply before moving into evolution and manifesting your highest potential.

Engage with the Reflection Prompts

After each affirmation, take time to reflect using the accompanying prompts.

These exercises are designed to help you uncover deeper insights and integrate the affirmations into your daily life. Use the journal space to document your thoughts and progress.

Incorporate the Mindful Practices

Towards the end of the book, you'll find additional tools to support your growth:
- A Forgiveness Letter exercise to release old burdens.
- A Letter to Your Higher Self to connect with your divine purpose.
- Daily Prayers to anchor your intentions and align with your highest good.

Be Consistent but Gentle with Yourself

Transformation is a journey, not a race. Progress at your own pace, and revisit sections as needed. This book is a resource you can return to whenever you need encouragement, clarity, or strength.

By using this book intentionally, you are not just reading—you're actively transforming. Embrace each step with love, patience, and gratitude. Your journey to healing and thriving starts now!

PART 1

Affirmations on Life's Ups and Downs

Discover Your Purpose, Embrace Your Power, and Heal Your Soul

I release the pain of the past and embrace the strength it has bestowed upon me.

Context:

Releasing pain may feel challenging, but it all comes down to how you choose to perceive it and move forward. Life's challenges aren't meant to break you—they're sent to help you grow. Embrace the lessons and don't let them weigh you down.

Reflection Prompt:

What pain are you ready to release, and what lessons has it taught you?

_____

_____

_____

_____

_____

_____

I trust that every challenge I face brings me closer to my purpose.

Context:

Every obstacle you encounter is a stepping stone toward discovering your true calling. Challenges aren't roadblocks; they are opportunities for growth, learning, and alignment with your higher purpose.

Reflection Prompt:

What is the biggest challenge you've faced recently, and how did you handle it?

_____

_____

_____

_____

_____

_____

_____

I embrace the flow of life, knowing that everything works for my highest good.

Context:

Trust that the universe has a plan for you. Even when things don't go as expected, they are guiding you closer to your highest potential. Life's flow may seem unpredictable, but it is leading you to where you need to be.

Reflection Prompt:

How do you typically react to setbacks, and how could you respond more positively?

_____

_____

_____

_____

_____

_____

Life's ups and downs are part of my evolution; I grow with every experience.

Context:

Life is a journey of growth. Each moment, whether challenging or joyful, serves as an essential part of your personal evolution. Embrace every experience as a lesson that contributes to your ongoing transformation.

Reflection Prompt:

What lessons have you learned from the difficult times in your life?

_____

_____

_____

_____

_____

_____

I am resilient and capable of navigating life's storms with grace.

Context:

Resilience isn't just about bouncing back from adversity; it's about handling it with calm, grace, and a steady belief in your inner strength. Life's storms will come, but you have the power to weather them with poise.

Reflection Prompt:

How can you remind yourself that life's downs are temporary and necessary for growth?

_____

_____

_____

_____

_____

_____

I release fear and trust that the universe has a plan for me.

Context:

Fear holds you back, but trust propels you forward. When you release fear, you create space for faith and belief in the universe's perfect timing. Trust that everything unfolding is for your highest good.

Reflection Prompt:

When life feels overwhelming, what self-care practices help you regain balance?

_____

_____

_____

_____

_____

_____

Every setback is a setup for an even greater comeback.

Context:

A setback is not the end but a redirection towards something greater. Use setbacks as fuel to propel yourself forward, knowing that each challenge brings you closer to an even greater opportunity.

Reflection Prompt:

How do you find joy and express gratitude, even during difficult times?

_____

_____

_____

_____

_____

_____

I am capable of transforming challenges into opportunities for growth.

Context:

Challenges are fertile ground for personal growth. When you face difficulties, seek the lessons within them. Every challenge carries the potential to make you stronger, wiser, and more capable.

Reflection Prompt:

What is one challenge you overcame that you thought was impossible?

_____

_____

_____

_____

_____

_____

_____

I trust the process, knowing that everything happens in divine timing.

Context:

Life is a journey, not a race. Trust the pace at which things unfold, knowing that everything happens at the right time, even when it's difficult to see in the moment.

Reflection Prompt:

How can you approach the ups and downs of life with greater resilience?

_____

_____

_____

_____

_____

_____

I am always supported by the universe, even during difficult times.

Context:

The universe supports you unconditionally. Even when times are tough, remember that you're never alone. Trust that you are being guided, protected, and supported through every challenge.

Reflection Prompt:

What role does your support system play in helping you through difficult times?

_____

_____

_____

_____

_____

_____

I embrace uncertainty with faith, knowing that it leads to new beginnings.

Context:

Uncertainty can feel unsettling, but it is a sign of new beginnings. Embrace the unknown with faith, knowing that it is leading you to something exciting and transformative. Do not let your circumstances define you.

Reflection Prompt:

How do you celebrate and honor your wins, no matter how small they may seem? If you don't, how can you start celebrating them?

_____

_____

_____

_____

_____

_____

PART 2

Affirmations on the Inner Child

Discover Your Purpose, Embrace Your Power,
and Heal Your Soul

I nurture and love my inner child with kindness and compassion.

Context:

Your inner child needs love, care, and attention. By nurturing this part of yourself, you heal old wounds and create a stronger foundation for personal growth. Be gentle and compassionate with your inner child.

Reflection Prompt:

What does your inner child need from you at this moment?

_____

_____

_____

_____

_____

_____

I embrace my inner child's innocence and creativity.

Context:

Your inner child embodies joy, wonder, and creativity. Embrace these qualities within yourself and allow them to inspire your life. Reconnect with the carefree, imaginative spirit of your youth.

Reflection Prompt:

What do you feel will bring you joy and creativity while doing it?

_____

_____

_____

_____

_____

_____

_____

I release any pain from my childhood and welcome healing.

Context:

Childhood experiences shape who we become, but they don't have to define us. By releasing childhood pain, you give your inner child the freedom to heal and move forward into a life of empowerment.

Reflection Prompt:

Which childhood memories still affect you, and how can you work through them?

_____

_____

_____

_____

_____

_____

I forgive my younger self and show it love and understanding.

Context:

Healing starts with forgiveness. Forgiving your younger self for past mistakes or hardships allows you to move forward with love and understanding. Your younger self did the best it could with the knowledge it had.

Reflection Prompt:

What would you say to your inner child if you could meet them face to face?

_____

_____

_____

_____

_____

_____

_____

I honor the wisdom my inner child offers me today.

Context:

Your inner child holds valuable wisdom: pure, honest, and full of joy. Honor the lessons your inner child has to offer, and allow those insights to shape your decisions and actions today.

Reflection Prompt:

How can you create a safe space within yourself to process old wounds?

_____

_____

_____

_____

_____

_____

I embrace playfulness and joy as I connect with my inner child.

Context:

Playfulness is a vital part of healing. Allow yourself to have fun, to be light-hearted, and to reconnect with the joy that comes from unburdening your spirit. Life doesn't always have to be serious; embrace the playful side of your nature.

Reflection Prompt:

What does healing look like for you, and how can you move towards it?

_____

_____

_____

_____

_____

_____

I am free to express my feelings and creativity as my true self.

Context:

Expressing yourself authentically is an important part of healing your inner child. Free yourself from the constraints of perfectionism and allow your true emotions and creativity to flow naturally.

Reflection Prompt:

How can you forgive yourself for the mistakes you have made in the past? How can you move forward by living authentically?

_____

_____

_____

_____

_____

_____

I honor my needs and care for my inner child with love and respect.

Context:

Your inner child has needs that must be met. By honoring these needs, whether they're emotional, creative, or physical, you help your inner child feel seen, heard, and loved.

Reflection Prompt:

How does your past affect the way that you show up in your relationships?

_____

_____

_____

_____

_____

_____

I protect my inner child by setting healthy boundaries.

Context:

Setting boundaries is an act of self-love and a way to protect your inner child. Safeguard this part of yourself from harmful situations or people while prioritizing your well-being.

Reflection Prompt:

What are some ways that you can start setting boundaries in your life now? What are some non-negotiable boundaries that you stand firm on?

_____

_____

_____

_____

_____

_____

_____

I embrace my inner child's vulnerability and give it a safe space to heal.

Context:

Vulnerability is part of healing. Create a safe space where your inner child can express its pain, fears, and needs without judgement. Embrace vulnerability as an essential step towards healing.

Reflection Prompt:

How can you celebrate your healing journey, even if it feels incomplete?

_____

_____

_____

_____

_____

_____

PART 3

Affirmations on Growth

Discover Your Purpose, Embrace Your Power,
and Heal Your Soul

Every day, I am becoming a better version of myself.

Context:

Growth is a continuous process. Each day offers an opportunity to become a better version of yourself. Celebrate the small improvements and trust that you're always evolving into your best self.

Reflection Prompt:

What does personal growth mean to you, and how do you measure it?

_____

_____

_____

_____

_____

_____

_____

I am committed to continuous personal growth and self-improvement.

Context:

Personal growth is a lifelong commitment. Stay dedicated to learning, growing, and improving yourself every day. The more committed you are to growth, the more you'll experience transformation.

Reflection Prompt:

How can you create a daily habit to foster growth and development?

_____

_____

_____

_____

_____

_____

I honor my journey and the lessons it brings.

Context:

Life is full of lessons, and each part of your journey is important. Honor your experiences, both good and bad, because they are shaping you into the person you are meant to be.

Reflection Prompt:

What steps can you take today to grow into the person you're meant to be?

_____

_____

_____

_____

_____

_____

I am open to new experiences that help me grow and expand.

Context:

Growth happens when you step outside your comfort zone. Be open to new experiences, ideas, and opportunities that allow you to expand and evolve. The unknown is where your greatest growth occurs.

Reflection Prompt:

What strengths have helped you overcome adversity in the past?

_____

_____

_____

_____

_____

_____

My growth is limitless, and I am always evolving.

Context:

There is no end to personal growth. You have unlimited potential and the ability to evolve continuously. Embrace the journey of becoming a better version of yourself each day.

Reflection Prompt:

When was the last time you felt proud of yourself, and why?

_____

_____

_____

_____

_____

_____

I trust in the process of transformation, knowing it leads to greatness.

Context:

Transformation is often messy and uncertain, but it is necessary for your growth. Trust that the process of change is leading you towards your highest potential, even when it feels uncomfortable.

Reflection Prompt:

What areas of your life are ready for growth?

_____

_____

_____

_____

_____

_____

I embrace change, knowing it's necessary for my personal growth.

Context:

Change can feel unsettling, but it's a powerful catalyst for growth. Embrace change as a natural part of your evolution. Every change moves you closer to the person you are meant to become.

Reflection Prompt:

How can you empower yourself to take the next step towards your goals?

_____

_____

_____

_____

_____

_____

I am not afraid of growth; I embrace it fully.

Context:

Growth requires courage. When you embrace growth, you step into new possibilities with excitement and open-mindedness. Don't fear the unknown; see it as an opportunity to become your best self.

Reflection Prompt:

What does personal success look like to you, and how can you get there?

_____

_____

_____

_____

_____

_____

Each challenge I face helps me grow stronger and wiser.

Context:

Every challenge is an opportunity for learning. With each struggle you encounter, you gain strength, wisdom, and resilience. Trust that these experiences are shaping you for greater things ahead.

Reflection Prompt:

When was the last time you stepped outside your comfort zone, and what did you learn?

_____

_____

_____

_____

_____

_____

I trust the timing of my growth, knowing it unfolds perfectly.

Context:

Growth takes time, and it unfolds at its own pace. Trust that everything is happening exactly when it's meant to. Be patient with yourself as you progress on your journey.

Reflection Prompt:

Do you honestly feel as if everything is always working out for you no matter what? Why or why not?

_____

_____

_____

_____

_____

_____

_____

PART 4

Affirmations on Trauma and Resilience

Discover Your Purpose, Embrace Your Power, and Heal Your Soul

I am resilient, and I grow stronger with every challenge I face.

Context:

Resilience is the ability to bounce back stronger after facing hardships. With each challenge, you become more equipped to handle adversity. Trust in your ability to rise stronger and more empowered.

Reflection Prompt:

What is one obstacle you overcame that you never thought you could?

_____

_____

_____

_____

_____

_____

I release the power trauma holds over me and take control of my healing.

Context:

Trauma may have shaped your past, but it does not define your future. By releasing its hold, you take back control of your healing journey and step into a place of empowerment and strength.

Reflection Prompt:

How have your challenges shaped the person you are today? How can you improve?

_____

_____

_____

_____

_____

_____

I am worthy of healing, and I embrace the process with courage.

Context:

Healing requires courage. By acknowledging that you are worthy of healing, you empower yourself to take the necessary steps towards emotional freedom and wholeness.

Reflection Prompt:

How can you view adversity as a chance to become stronger and wiser?

_____

_____

_____

_____

_____

_____

I am not my trauma. I am a survivor, and I choose to live fully.

Context:

This encourages you to let go of the weight of your past and step into your power. It's a reminder that you are stronger than what you've been through, and you have the courage to create a life filled with joy, healing, and purpose. Your past doesn't define you; your choice to live fully does!

Reflection Prompt:

When have you felt held back by your past, and how can you choose to move forward with strength and purpose today?

_____

_____

_____

_____

_____

_____

I release fear and step into the light of my true self.

Context:

Fear often keeps us stuck in the past, but by releasing it, we allow ourselves to step into the fullness of who we are. Embrace the light of your true self, free from fear and limitations.

Reflection Prompt:

How can you replace fear with faith and take the leap?

_____

_____

_____

_____

_____

_____

I am grateful for my strength and resilience during difficult times.

Context:

Gratitude for your resilience helps you recognize the inner strength that has carried you through. Every challenge faced builds your strength and deepens your appreciation for your ability to persevere.

Reflection Prompt:

What tools or habits can you develop to build resilience over time?

_____

_____

_____

_____

_____

_____

I trust in my ability to heal and move forward with confidence.

Context:

Healing is a process, and you can trust that you have the ability to move through it with confidence. Every step forward brings you closer to emotional freedom and peace.

Reflection Prompt:

How can you see healing as a lifelong journey rather than a destination?

_____

_____

_____

_____

_____

_____

I choose to break free from the chains of my past and embrace a brighter future.

Context:

The past does not have to dictate your future. By choosing to break free from past limitations, you create a space for a new, brighter chapter filled with limitless possibilities.

Reflection Prompt:

How can you forgive yourself for your past? What steps can you take today to release the past and move toward the future you deserve?

_____

_____

_____

_____

_____

_____

I am deserving of peace and happiness, regardless of my past experiences.

Context:

Your past does not determine your worth. You are deserving of peace and happiness, and you have the right to experience joy, no matter what you've been through.

Reflection Prompt:

What unresolved emotions might be holding you back, and how can you release them?

_____

_____

_____

_____

_____

_____

I embrace my healing journey with patience, love, and trust.

Context:

Healing takes time, and it's a journey that requires patience and love. Trust that every step you take is a step towards peace and wholeness. Treat yourself with the same kindness and care you would offer a loved one on their healing journey.

Reflection Prompt:

How can you create space in your life for emotional healing and growth?

_____

_____

_____

_____

_____

_____

PART 5

Affirmations on Healing

Discover Your Purpose, Embrace Your Power, and Heal Your Soul

I release past hurts and choose to heal in this moment.

Context:

Healing begins when you decide to release past wounds and let go of old hurts. Every day offers a new opportunity to heal, and choosing to do so frees you to move forward with peace and clarity.

Reflection Prompt:

How can you be more gentle with yourself as you heal from past experiences?

_____

_____

_____

_____

_____

_____

I am worthy of love, healing, and happiness.

Context:

Healing starts with acknowledging your inherent worth. You are deserving of all the love, healing, and joy that life has to offer. Open yourself to receive these gifts, knowing you are worthy of them.

Reflection Prompt:

How can you release old patterns and embrace healing in your life?

_____

_____

_____

_____

_____

_____

I forgive myself and others, allowing healing to flow freely.

Context:

Forgiveness is an essential part of the healing process. When you release resentment and anger, you create space for healing and peace to enter your life. Forgiveness frees you to live without the burden of the past.

Reflection Prompt:

What does it mean for you to fully forgive yourself and others?

_____

_____

_____

_____

_____

_____

_____

I trust my body's ability to heal and restore balance.

Context:

Your body is incredibly resilient. Trust that it knows how to heal itself when you nurture it properly. By cultivating trust in your body's natural healing abilities, you empower it to restore balance and vitality.

Reflection Prompt:

How can you start letting go of old emotional wounds that no longer serve you?

_____

_____

_____

_____

_____

_____

I am in the process of becoming whole, healthy, and healed.

Context:

Healing is a journey, and you are in the process of becoming whole. Every step you take towards healing brings you closer to a healthier and more balanced version of yourself. Trust the process.

Reflection Prompt:

What are some things you can do to nurture your healing journey on a daily basis?

_____

_____

_____

_____

_____

_____

_____

I honor my feelings and give myself permission to heal at my own pace.

Context:

Healing doesn't happen overnight, and there is no 'right' timeline. Honor your feelings and give yourself permission to move at your own pace. Each moment of self-compassion contributes to your healing.

Reflection Prompt:

Do you feel any pressures to heal on a certain timeline, and how can you release them to honor your own pace?

_____

_____

_____

_____

_____

_____

I am letting go of emotional pain, making space for peace and joy.

Context:

Emotional pain can be heavy, but releasing it makes room for peace and joy. Allow yourself to let go of what no longer serves you, knowing that healing creates space for positivity and new beginnings.

Reflection Prompt:

In what ways can you show love and compassion to yourself today? What is something you want to release that doesn't serve you anymore?

_____

_____

_____

_____

_____

_____

I am grateful for my body's ability to heal and restore itself.

Context:

Gratitude for your body's natural healing process helps accelerate recovery. Appreciate the amazing way your body restores balance and supports you through every challenge, both physical and emotional.

Reflection Prompt:

Write down three things that you are grateful for and explain why in detail.

_____

_____

_____

_____

_____

_____

Healing is a choice, and I choose to embrace it fully.

Context:

Healing begins with a decision. By choosing to embrace healing, you take control of your emotional and physical well-being. Trust that every choice to heal is a powerful step toward renewal.

Reflection Prompt:

What does taking control of your life mean to you? In what ways can you show up for yourself?

_____

_____

_____

_____

_____

_____

I am patient and compassionate with myself as I heal.

Context:

Healing requires patience and self-compassion. Be gentle with yourself, understanding that healing is not a linear process. Enjoy your journey, and evolve as you learn.

Reflection Prompt:

How can you embrace change, rather than resisting it?

_____

_____

_____

_____

_____

_____

PART 6

Affirmations on Confidence

Discover Your Purpose, Embrace Your Power, and Heal Your Soul

I am confident in my ability to create the life I desire.

Context:

Confidence begins with belief in your own power. You have the ability to manifest and shape the life of your dreams. Trust that you are capable of achieving anything you set your mind to.

Reflection Prompt:

What does true confidence mean to you?

_____

_____

_____

_____

_____

_____

I radiate self-assurance and trust in my worth.

Context:

True confidence comes from within. By recognizing your own worth and standing tall in your truth, you emit a powerful energy that attracts success, love, and opportunities.

Reflection Prompt:

In which areas of your life do you feel most empowered?

_____

_____

_____

_____

_____

_____

I am proud of who I am and the progress I've made.

Context:

Celebrate your progress, no matter how small. You have come a long way on your journey, recognizing that growth builds confidence and a deeper sense of self-worth.

Reflection Prompt:

When was the last time you felt proud of yourself, and why?

_____

_____

_____

_____

_____

_____

I trust my intuition to guide me towards my highest potential.

Context:

Your intuition is a powerful tool that can lead you in the right direction. Trust it, and let it guide you to decisions that align with your highest potential. Your inner wisdom knows what is best for you.

Reflection Prompt:

Can you recall a scenario where you ignored your intuition? What was the outcome, and what did you learn from the experience?

_____

_____

_____

_____

_____

_____

_____

My confidence grows with each step I take towards my goals.

Context:

Confidence is built through action. Every small step you take towards your goals strengthens your self-belief. Trust that each effort, no matter how small, is bringing you closer to the life you desire.

Reflection Prompt:

What qualities do you admire in confident people, and how can you embody them?

_____

_____

_____

_____

_____

_____

_____

I believe in my abilities and embrace my uniqueness.

Context:

Your abilities and individuality are your strengths. Embrace what makes you unique, and trust in your talents. Believing in your skills will help you confidently move towards your dreams.

Reflection Prompt:

What abilities and characteristics make you unique? What do you love about yourself?

_____

_____

_____

_____

_____

_____

I am a magnet for success and opportunities.

Context:

Confidence attracts opportunities. When you believe in your ability to succeed, you naturally draw success and opportunities into your life. Trust that your confidence creates a magnetic energy that brings abundance.

Reflection Prompt:

What opportunities do you think confidence could attract for you over the next six months?

_____

_____

_____

_____

_____

_____

I stand tall in my truth and speak with clarity and confidence.

Context:

Speak your truth with conviction. Confidence comes from knowing who you are and standing firm in your beliefs. When you communicate with clarity and confidence, you inspire respect and trust.

Reflection Prompt:

If you embodied unshakeable confidence every day, how would your life change?

_____

_____

_____

_____

_____

_____

_____

I love and accept myself fully, and others mirror that love.

Context:

The way you love and accept yourself sets the tone for how others treat you. By cultivating deep self-love and acceptance, you create an environment where others reflect that same love back to you.

Reflection Prompt:

What does loving yourself unconditionally look like for you?

_____

_____

_____

_____

_____

_____

My confidence empowers me to overcome any obstacle in my path.

Context:

Confidence is the key to overcoming obstacles. When you believe in yourself, no challenge seems overwhelming. You have the inner strength to tackle whatever life throws at you with courage and determination.

Reflection Prompt:

How do you handle setbacks or criticism while staying confident? How could you?

_____

_____

_____

_____

_____

_____

PART 7

Affirmations on Evolving

Discover Your Purpose, Embrace Your Power, and Heal Your Soul

I trust my ability to grow, evolve, and adapt to life's changes.

Context:

Growth is a constant and natural part of life. Trust that you have the ability to evolve, learn, and adapt to whatever comes your way. Every challenge is an opportunity for growth.

Reflection Prompt:

What part of your journey are you most proud of, and why?

_____

_____

_____

_____

_____

_____

I choose to focus on what I can control and release what I cannot.

Context:

Focus your energy on what you can control—your thoughts, actions, and mindset. Release the things you cannot control and trust that by letting go, you make room for growth and peace.

Reflection Prompt:

What's holding you back from fully embracing who you are?

_____

_____

_____

_____

_____

_____

I believe in my limitless potential and take bold steps toward my dreams.

Context:

Your potential is limitless, and you are capable of achieving anything you set your mind to. Believe in yourself and take bold, confident steps toward creating your dreams, knowing that you have everything you need to succeed.

Reflection Prompt:

What's a risk you've been avoiding, and how could taking it help you grow?

_____

_____

_____

_____

_____

_____

I am constantly learning, unlearning, and relearning to align with my highest self.

Context:

Evolution isn't linear; it's a cycle of acquiring new knowledge, letting go of old patterns, and embracing fresh perspectives.

Reflection Prompt:

What's something you've recently unlearned that has helped you grow?

_____

_____

_____

_____

_____

_____

Each day, I grow closer to the life I desire by staying committed to my vision.

Context:

Consistency is key to personal evolution. This reinforces that small, intentional steps every day lead to significant transformations.

Reflection Prompt:

What's one daily habit you can commit to that aligns with your higher self?

_____

_____

_____

_____

_____

_____

I am a magnet for success, abundance, and opportunities.

Context:

By aligning with your highest self, you attract success, abundance, and opportunities into your life. Your energy and mindset create a magnetic force that draws in all that you desire.

Reflection Prompt:

What are some of your desires that you are trying to attract? What does having your desires mean to you?

_____

_____

_____

_____

_____

_____

I let go of fear and doubt, replacing them with unwavering belief in myself.

Context:

Fear and doubt hold you back from your true potential. Let go of these limiting beliefs and replace them with a deep, unwavering belief in yourself and your abilities. You are capable of achieving greatness.

Reflection Prompt:

What are some of your current fears, and how are they holding you back? How can you encourage yourself to overcome your fears?

_____

_____

_____

_____

_____

_____

I am deserving of success and trust that it is on its way to me.

Context:

Success is already on its way to you. Trust in your ability to achieve your goals, and know that your hard work and dedication are bringing you closer to the success you deserve.

Reflection Prompt:

What can you do today to move closer to your most abundant life?

_____

_____

_____

_____

_____

_____

I am a powerful creator, and I am constantly evolving into the best version of myself.

Context:

You have the power to create the life you desire. As you evolve and grow, continue to refine your skills, mindset, and actions to become the best version of yourself. Your potential is ever-expanding.

Reflection Prompt:

What beliefs about money and success do you need to shift?

_____

_____

_____

_____

_____

_____

I am proud of how far I've come and excited for where I am going.

Context:

Celebrate your growth and the progress you've made. Be proud of how far you've come, and look forward with excitement to the incredible future you are creating.

Reflection Prompt:

How have past experiences shaped your beliefs, and how can you reframe them?

_____

_____

_____

_____

_____

_____

PART 8

Affirmations on Manifesting Your Dream Life

Discover Your Purpose, Embrace Your Power, and Heal Your Soul

I am worthy of living my dream life, and I take inspired action towards it.

Context:

Your dream life is not out of reach; it is already yours to claim. Trust that you are worthy of everything you desire and take inspired action every day to manifest your dreams into reality.

Reflection Prompt:

What does your dream life look like, and how can you start living it now?

_____

_____

_____

_____

_____

_____

I attract everything I need to create the life I've always dreamed of.

Context:

The universe is always conspiring in your favor. Trust that everything you need to build your dream life is already on its way to you, and be open to receiving it.

Reflection Prompt:

How do you feel when you imagine manifesting abundance and luxury?

_____

_____

_____

_____

_____

_____

I am a powerful manifester, and I effortlessly attract the energy I desire.

Context:

Manifestation is a natural process that flows through you. Trust your ability to attract the energy, people, and opportunities that align with your desires. You are a powerful manifester.

Reflection Prompt:

How can you create a mindset of abundance to attract your dream life?

_____

_____

_____

_____

_____

_____

I am aligned with my higher self, and my dreams are already coming true.

Context:

When you align with your higher self, everything you desire falls into place. Trust that your dreams are already on their way to you as you remain in alignment with your purpose.

Reflection Prompt:

What does true abundance mean to you, and how do you recognize it?

_____

_____

_____

_____

_____

_____

I release limiting beliefs and open myself to limitless possibilities.

Context:

Limiting beliefs block the flow of abundance. Let go of these beliefs and open yourself to limitless possibilities. The universe is abundant, and you are worthy of receiving all it has to offer.

Reflection Prompt:

In what ways can you take a step towards eliminating self-doubt? Make a small list of your limiting beliefs, then rewrite your limiting belief to something positive and empowering.

_____

_____

_____

_____

_____

_____

I deserve to live a life of luxury, and I am open to receiving it.

Context:

You are deserving of a life of luxury and abundance. Open yourself to receiving all the blessings, wealth, and joy that life has to offer. Allow yourself to enjoy the fruits of your manifestations.

Reflection Prompt:

What steps can you take to open yourself up to the flow of abundance?

_____

_____

_____

_____

_____

_____

I am the architect of my life, and I design it with love, passion, and purpose.

Context:

You are in control of your life's design. Take charge of your future and create the life you've always dreamed of, filled with love, passion, and purpose. You are the creator of your destiny.

Reflection Prompt:

What qualities do you associate with living a luxurious, fulfilled life? What do you feel your purpose is, and how can you embody it?

_____

_____

_____

_____

_____

_____

I attract opportunities that align with my highest purpose and desires.

Context:

Opportunities are constantly presenting themselves to you. By staying aligned with your highest purpose, you attract those opportunities that will help you achieve your dreams.

Reflection Prompt:

How can you align your actions with your desires for success and abundance?

_____

_____

_____

_____

_____

_____

I trust the timing of my life, knowing that everything unfolds as it should.

Context:

Trust that everything is unfolding in divine timing. Even if things don't happen as quickly as you'd like, know that everything is falling into place exactly as it should.

Reflection Prompt:

How can you begin living as if your dreams have already come true?

_____

_____

_____

_____

_____

_____

I am grateful for the abundance I already have, and I am ready to receive more.

Context:

Gratitude is the key to unlocking more abundance in your life. Be grateful for what you already have, and trust that more blessings are on their way to you.

Reflection Prompt:

What are you grateful for in your life right now? How can you open yourself to receive even more abundance?

_____

_____

_____

_____

_____

_____

PART 9

Affirmations on Holistic Living and Self-Care

Discover Your Purpose, Embrace Your Power, and Heal Your Soul

I honor the balance between my mind, body, and spirit by nurturing all aspects of my being.

Context:

Holistic living involves recognizing that your mental, physical, and spiritual health are interconnected. By making time to care for each aspect, you create harmony in your life.

Reflection Prompt:

How do you currently nurture your mind, body, and spirit?

_____

_____

_____

_____

_____

_____

_____

I give myself permission to rest and recharge because my well-being matters.

Context:

In a world that often celebrates constant productivity, it's easy to forget the importance of rest. Prioritizing rest isn't laziness; it's self-preservation. This affirmation encourages you to view rest as an essential part of your self-care routine, helping you to stay energized and resilient.

Reflection Prompt:

What signs does your body or mind give you when you need to slow down? How can you create a safe space for yourself to unwind without guilt?

_____

_____

_____

_____

_____

_____

I choose nourishing foods and activities that fuel my energy and vitality.

Context:

The choices you make each day directly impact how you feel physically and emotionally. Eating wholesome foods, staying hydrated, and energized in activities that uplift you can improve your overall health.

Reflection Prompt:

What foods or activities make you feel most energized and alive?

_____

_____

_____

_____

_____

_____

_____

I release the need for perfection and embrace the beauty of progress in my self-care journey.

Context:

Self-care isn't about perfection; it's about meeting yourself where you are and making sustainable improvements. It's essential to let go of pressure and instead focus on taking small meaningful steps.

Reflection Prompt:

In what ways do you put unnecessary pressure on yourself in your self-care routine? What does progress—not perfection—look like for you?

_____

_____

_____

_____

_____

_____

I protect my peace by setting healthy boundaries and honoring my needs.

Context:

Protecting your mental and emotional well-being requires boundaries. Whether it's saying no to over commitments or limiting time with draining people, honoring your needs demonstrates self-respect.

Reflection Prompt:

What boundaries can you set to protect your energy and peace?

_____

_____

_____

_____

_____

_____

I create a life of balance by prioritizing what truly matters to me.

Context:

Life can feel chaotic when you lose sight of your priorities. This affirmation serves as a guide to focus on what brings you joy, fulfilment, and alignment, rather than being swept up in external demands.

Reflection Prompt:

What are the top three things that matter most to you in life?

_____

_____

_____

_____

_____

_____

I am deeply connected to nature and find healing in its rhythms and beauty.

Context:

Nature is a powerful tool for healing and grounding. Spending time outdoors, feeling the earth beneath your feet, or simply appreciating the beauty of a sunset can recharge your spirit.

Reflection Prompt:

How often do you spend time in nature, and how does it make you feel? How can you incorporate more outdoor time into your daily or weekly routine?

_____

_____

_____

_____

_____

_____

I listen to my body's wisdom and honor what it needs in the moment.

Context:

Your body constantly communicates with you, whether through fatigue, hunger, or tension. Learning to listen to its cues and responding with care is a foundational act of self-care.

Reflection Prompt:

How can you build trust in your body's ability to guide you toward well-being? Are there times when you ignore your body's signals, and why?

_____

_____

_____

_____

_____

_____

I attract peace and joy by cultivating gratitude and positivity in my daily life.

Context:

Gratitude and positivity are powerful forces that can shift your energy and perspective. It's important to focus on what's good in your life, fostering a mindset of abundance and peace.

Reflection Prompt:

How do you typically handle negativity, and how can you shift towards positivity?

_____

_____

_____

_____

_____

_____

I embrace self-care as an act of love, not as an obligation.

Context:

Self-care isn't just something to check off a list—it's an intentional act of love and kindness towards yourself. See self-care as something to enjoy and look forward to, rather than a chore.

Reflection Prompt:

What self-care practices make you feel genuinely nurtured and valued?

_____

_____

_____

_____

_____

_____

MINDFUL PRACTICES

What are mindful practices?

Mindful practices are intentional actions that help you stay present, cultivate self-awareness, and nurture your mental, emotional, and spiritual well-being. These practices encourage you to slow down, reflect, and connect with the present moment, allowing you to engage with life in a more meaningful way. They can include meditation, journaling, deep breathing, gratitude exercises, affirmations, or any activity that promotes a sense of calm and clarity.

Types of Practices

- Meditation is the practice of sitting in stillness and focusing on your breath, a mantra, or a visualization to cultivate inner peace and clarity. It helps reduce stress, improve focus, and enhance self-awareness.

- Gratitude Journaling involves writing down things you're thankful for daily. This shifts your focus from what's lacking to what's abundant in your life, promoting a positive mindset.

- Deep Breathing Exercises are intentional breathing techniques that calm your nervous system. They help reduce stress and bring you into the present moment.

- Affirmation is the practice of repeating positive, empowering statements to shift your mindset, overcome self-doubt, and manifest your desires.

- Body Scanning is a meditative practice where you focus on each part of your body, releasing tension and increasing both physical and emotional awareness.

- Visualization involves creating a mental image of your desired outcomes. This practice strengthens your belief in achieving your goals and attracts positive energy.

- Walking Meditation is the practice of walking slowly and intentionally while focusing on the sensations of movement and your surroundings. It grounds you and improves focus.

- Grounding Exercises are activities, like walking barefoot on grass or holding natural elements, that help you reconnect with the Earth and reduce stress.

- Journaling for Reflection involves writing down your thoughts and emotions to process experiences, release negativity, and gain clarity.

- Yoga or Stretching consists of moving your body in a mindful way to release tension, build strength, and connect with your breath.

- Gratitude Letters are heartfelt letters written to someone you appreciate. This practice strengthens relationships and promotes a positive outlook.

- Mindful Decluttering is the act of clearing your space while focusing on the emotions and intentions behind each item you choose to keep or discard.

- Mindful Coloring or Drawing involves engaging in creative activities that relax your mind and encourage self-expression.

- Digital Detox is taking breaks from screens to reduce mental clutter and increase your presence in the physical environment.

- Energy Cleansing includes practices like smudging with sage or using crystals to release negative energy and restore balance.

- Daily Intention Setting is the act of declaring a focus or goal for the day to align your actions with your higher purpose.

- Creating a Vision Board involves using images and words to represent your goals, reinforcing your focus on manifesting them.

- Inner Child Connection includes engaging in activities your younger self loved or writing a letter to your inner child to heal and nurture that part of you.

- Mindful Music Listening is tuning into the lyrics, melody, and rhythm to fully experience the emotions and messages conveyed by the music.

- Nightly Reflections involves reviewing your day with compassion, noting successes and areas for improvement without judgment.

- Loving-Kindness Meditation is sending thoughts of love and goodwill to yourself and others to foster connection and reduce negative emotions.

FORGIVENESS LETTERS

Write a letter to yourself, forgiving past mistakes, regrets, or moments of self-judgement. Then, write a letter to someone else you feel the need to forgive, releasing resentment, and choosing peace.

_____

_____

_____

_____

_____

_____

_____

_____

LETTER TO YOUR HIGHER SELF

Write a letter to your higher self, expressing your dreams, fears, and gratitude. Ask for guidance, clarity, and strength to align with your highest purpose. Keep this letter as a reminder of your connection to your true essence and your journey towards growth.

_____

_____

_____

_____

_____

_____

_____

_____

_____

_____

ESSENTIAL PRAYERS

RISING PRAYER

Gracious soul, I awaken to a new day filled with divine potential. Thank you for this breath and the gift of life anew. Guide my thoughts, words, and actions so that I may walk in alignment with love, grace, and purpose. May I be a vessel of light and kindness, radiating joy and attracting blessings in all forms. I set my intentions with faith, and I trust that you are leading me on a path of abundance, peace, and growth. I am grateful, I am whole, and I am ready. So it is, so it shall be.

NIGHT PRAYER

Divine Source of light and love, as I lay down to rest, I surrender all the weight of this day. Wrap me in your infinite peace, protecting me through the stillness of the night. May my dreams be sacred and my spirit rejuvenated, aligning with the highest vibrations of love, wisdom, and healing. I release all worries and open my heart to your loving embrace. Thank you for the blessings, seen and unseen, that surround me. I rest in the knowing that I am safe, cherished, and divinely guided. So it is, so it shall be.

MEAL PRAYER

Dear Divine Source of nourishment, thank you for this food before me, a gift of abundance and life. I am grateful for the hands and hearts that brought it to my table, for the earth that provided it, and for the love and care that sustain me through it. May this food bring me strength, health, and joy. May it nourish my body, mind, and spirit, and fill me with energy and gratitude. I honor this meal, knowing it is a blessing from the Divine, and I receive it with love and appreciation. So it is, so it shall be.

SELF LOVE PRAYER

Dear Divine Source, I open my heart to embrace myself fully, with love, kindness, and compassion. I honor who I am, knowing I am worthy, valuable, and deserving of all good things. I release any doubts, criticisms, and judgments that I have held against myself and replace them with acceptance and appreciation. May I see myself through the eyes of love, approving of my unique journey, and trusting that I am enough just as I am. I am grateful for the strength, wisdom, and beauty within me, and I allow self-love to flow freely in my life. So it is, so it shall be.

FAITH PRAYER

Dear Divine Source, I trust that everything in my life is unfolding perfectly for my highest good. I release any worries or doubts and allow myself to rest in the assurance that all is well. I believe in the divine timing and guidance that surrounds me, knowing that every challenge brings me closer to my dreams. Thank you for aligning my path with joy, peace, and success. I affirm that everything always works out for me, and I am exactly where I need to be. So it is, so it shall be.

OVERCOMING OBSTACLES PRAYER

Dear Divine Source, I call upon your infinite power to guide me through every obstacle with unwavering strength and unshakable faith. Fill me with clarity, resilience, and the courage to rise above all challenges. Transform every setback into a stepping stone toward my highest purpose. Surround me with your light and align me with your divine plan, for I am unstoppable and victorious. So it is, so it shall be.

FULFILLING SOUL'S PURPOSE PRAYER

Dear Divine Source, I open my heart and spirit to your guidance as I seek to align with my soul's true purpose. I trust that I am here for a reason, and I am ready to fulfill the unique calling that you have placed within me. Help me to recognize the signs, passions, and gifts that lead me along my path, and to pursue them with courage, clarity, and faith. May I be a vessel for love, wisdom, and kindness, sharing my gifts with the world in ways that bring light and healing. I ask for the strength to overcome any doubts or fears and for the wisdom to stay true to my path, even when it's challenging. Thank you for the purpose you have placed within me. I am ready to fulfill it with an open heart, knowing I am guided and supported every step of the way. So it is, so it shall be.

HEALTHY RELATIONSHIP PRAYER

Dear Divine Source, Thank you for the gift of love in my life and for the beautiful connection I share with my partner. I ask for guidance to keep our relationship strong, balanced, and filled with mutual respect, understanding, and joy. May our love continue to grow, rooted in honesty, trust, and open communication. Help us to support one another's growth and dreams, and to be a source of comfort, strength, and inspiration for each other. May our relationship be a reflection of Divine love, bringing peace, happiness, and harmony to our lives. I am grateful for this partnership, and I nurture it with gratitude and care. So it is, so it shall be.

WEALTH PRAYER

Dear Divine Source of all abundance, open my heart and mind to the infinite blessings that surround me. I release any thoughts of lack or fear and welcome prosperity in every form.

I align my soul with the energy of wealth, knowing that I am worthy of receiving it effortlessly. I trust that money flows to me with ease, providing me with all that I need and more. Abundance is my birthright, and I gratefully accept it, letting it enrich my life and those around me.

With every breath, I draw in the energy of prosperity, and with every exhale, I release any barriers within me. I call forth financial abundance, peace, and security, trusting that my needs are always met. May my dreams be a sanctuary for guidance, showing me the path to wealth and fulfillment.

Thank you for blessing me with the power to manifest my desires. I am open, I am grateful, and I am ready to receive. So it is, so it shall be!

ABOUT THE AUTHOR

Ariyanna is an entrepreneur with over a decade of experience, navigating the highs and lows of life with grace and resilience. Having overcome countless hurdles, she has discovered the power of healing, personal growth, and stepping boldly into her authenticity.

Ariyanna is deeply passionate about helping others heal, align with their true selves, and embrace their inner strength. She believes that growth is possible for anyone, and is dedicated to inspiring others to walk confidently in their power. Her work is grounded in the values of personal development, authenticity, and living a purposeful life.

Through her journey, Ariyanna continues to encourage others to embrace transformation and create lives filled with intention, joy, and fulfilment.

A HEARTFELT THANK YOU

I want to take a moment to express my deepest gratitude for choosing this book and supporting the vision behind it. By making this purchase, you've invested in your growth, healing, and alignment, and for that, I am endlessly proud of you. This is more than just a book; it's a tool, a companion, and a safe space for you to evolve into your highest self.

Congratulations in advance for all the incredible accomplishments, breakthroughs, and successes waiting for you on this journey. Know that you are already amazing, and even more incredible things are unfolding for you now and forever.

Thank you for trusting me to be part of your transformation. May this book serve as a constant reminder of your strength, resilience, and divine power. You are capable, you are deserving, and you are unstoppable.

With love and gratitude,
Ariyanna

Printed in Dunstable, United Kingdom